Aquamarine

Also by Michele Fermanis-Winward
and published by Ginninderra Press

Threading Raindrops
The Eucalypt Distillery
A Larrikin in the Blood
These Weighted Months
The Symbiotic Web
To the Dam (Pocket Poets)
The Sail Weaver (Pocket Poets)
Curdled Milk (Pocket Poets)

Michele Fermanis-Winward

Aquamarine

Acknowledgements

With gratitude to my editor Brendan Doyle, for his continued enthusiasm and support. A Varuna Writer's Space Fellowship developed many of the poems in this collection.

'Salt on the Skin' first appeared in *The Crow*, 'Poetry Journal' and 'Jellyfish' in *Add to Cart Magazine* and the *Mounted ARI Project*.

I offer special thanks to my publishers, Stephen Matthews OAM and Brenda Eldridge for their hard work and devotion to the independent voice.

I live and work on the unceded lands of the Yaluk-ut Weelam of the Boon Wurrung and the Darug and Gundungurra people. I pay my respects to these traditional owners and to elders past and present.

I dedicate this collection to my husband,
Kevin Fermanis-Winward,
for his love and indefatigable encouragement.

Aquamarine
ISBN 978 1 76109 524 5
Copyright © text Michele Fermanis-Winward 2023
Cover image: Michele Fermanis-Winward

First published 2023 by
GINNINDERRA PRESS
PO Box 3461 Port Adelaide 5015
www.ginninderrapress.com.au

Contents

Introduction	9
In Two Worlds	
Pre-Cambrian	13
The Labyrinth of Time	14
The Mysteries	15
Bridging Time	16
Wreckage	17
The Invaders	18
Macquarie Harbour	19
Picking Oakum	20
Through the Spyglass	21
The Siren	22
Selkie Skin	23
At Shippies	25
Ghosts	26
The Treasure Hunter	27
Catani Gardens	28
Anzac Day	30
Rye Back Beach	31
Survival Instinct	32
Sand Between the Sheets	
Luminous	35
Bella At Large	36
Opening Up, November 2021	37
Luna Land	38
St Kilda Summertime	39
Bayside Vignette	41
Acland Street Symphony	42
The Crime of Innocence	43

On Ebb Tide	44
Urban Penguins	45
Black Swan	46
At the Turn	47
In Homage	48
Yachts	49
Flightless Birds	50
Painting the Morning	51
Bright Bella	52
Salt on the Skin	53
Homesong	54

Waterworn

The Riverside Path	57
The River of Cloud	58
Nowhere to Run	59
La Serenissima Protests	60
Yesterday's Ocean	61
Jellyfish	62
The Lone Sailor	63
The Grindadrap	64
Mohad's Anniversary	65
From Her Window	66
Hermit Rocks	67
Through Another Art	68
Big Rivers	69
The Ugly Duckling Tree	70
The Tropic of Contrasts	71
This Moment, a Breath	72
Sea Steps	73

Listing to Port
- Aquamarine   77
- Time Share   78
- Sunday Notebook   80
- Basking   81
- Friday's Beach   83
- At Shelly Beach   84
- Stepping Into Shadows   85
- The Stations of My Day   86
- Entering the Depths   87
- The Sighting   88
- Echoes   89
- Oriole   90
- Heart to Heart   91
- Waterborne   92
- Bench Marks   93
- Ozone   94
- Love Token   95

Introduction

I grew up in bayside Melbourne a short walk from the local beach. As a family, we gathered periwinkles and mussels for Sunday lunch, we swam with stingrays and explored rock pools at Ricketts Point. In summer, primary school lunchtime was a picnic on the beach; our school swimming carnivals were held at the open-air Brighton and St Kilda baths. My parents loved the ocean. We had a plot of land at Rye along the Victorian coast, then as teenagers a holiday house at Queenscliff, going to the fishermen's wharf each Sunday for fresh-caught shellfish.

Today, I divide my time between mountain-top Blackheath in the clouds, my husband's soul country, and St Kilda by the bay. My longed-for annual break these last thirty years has been to Port Macquarie, where I can wake each morning to the sound of waves. This collection is for my love of Aquamarine, the water of the sea.

In Two Worlds

Pre-Cambrian

Evolved beyond bacteria
we fed on slime
four billions years ago
how strange to think of us this way

our soft bodied forebears
filtering the ocean bed
before this world of bone and shell
the age of calcium began

we were these leaf shaped worms
blind, fragile, multicelled
clinging to our shallow sea
as the climate warmed and froze

overpowered and lost from sight
until a book of stone revealed
the story fossils hold
and brings our ancestors home.

The Labyrinth of Time

The sound of waves
its constant roar
the pulse of infinite power
a lifeline out of Africa
towards our furthest home

the ocean stretches
beyond imagination
it cradles lives as yet unknown
the microscopic simple-celled
and the greatest whale

we strode its shores
into new lands
emboldened by our minds
the songs we made
to combat dark and death

tsunamis
sweep us from the earth
islands drown and floods destroy
but still we clasp the shore
as the mother of us all.

The Mysteries

Mist obscures where sky and sea align
between the coast and lost horizon's edge
a humpback whale whispers to her calf
'stay close, be safe, have milk'

dolphins play, surf random waves
while small fish hide and seek
breakers rush, they push and suck
thrust their sibilance on sand

they arabesque across the beach
write messages for gulls to scour
in seagrass weighed by fruits
which ooze and burst, disgorge

the remnant trails of lives unseen
form pictures in our heads
the marvels of another world
so close and yet unknown.

Bridging Time

Lands End in Cornwall
here we stand
beneath the soft churn of a wind turbine
pulsing like a heartbeat

among the yellow gorse
we find a standing stone
its face worn down by lost millennia
looking out to sea, to guide a sail
safely back in shore

they coexist
this symbol of an ancient race
its mystery and our technology
steadfast before the wind.

Wreckage

How long
for you to slip away
to lose the light
anchored as you were

your skin to peel
and fish to reach your bones
reduced to remnant parts
at peace within the sand

the sluice of tides reveals
a fragment of your life
washed to a distant beach
among its rocks and weed

the ring and bolt
that weighed you down
rusted, shell-encrusted
eloquent as the hour
they chained you in the hold.

The Invaders

The sky hangs low upon the sea
this place of cold, eating to the bone
our steps unheard upon the sand
not the shingles of our home
that rattle if we're stalked

the naturals of this land
plump infants in their arms
feast and dance oblivious to need
they fear our guns and knives
the murder in our hearts

they forage from the coast
hunt game with spears and sticks
how easy they survive
while we drag our chains
are flogged and starve

some of us escape
blind fools we're ill equipped
strike inland and are lost
we fall upon our friends
and turn them into meat.

Macquarie Harbour

Here I bought a porridge spoon
of golden huon pine
with a scent to charm my nose
but I felt the past envelop me
deep sorrow welled inside

this place of rain and cold
with timber prized for ships
its history of penal law
with no redemptive hope
just unrelenting toil

half starved and flogged
prisoners worked till they fell
in freezing wet all day
my forebear suffered here
among those wretched men

I walk the island ruins
pay homage to John Avery
he submitted and endured
the reason I am here today
stirring milk and oats.

Picking Oakum

Inside the female factory walls
she finds a patch of sun
bends over lengths of rope
jumbled on the ground
her quota for the day

with fingers blacked
and lungs that wheeze
on fibre shreds, she picks
at tar and salty strands
unwinds what years
of sea have fused

she flinches at the sight
of ghost white birds
with taunting cries
they freely come and go
while she unravels
and is bound.

Through the Spyglass

I crest the hill
and catch myself surprised
black masts and spars
set against a sun dazed sea
like coastal sailing ships
riding at the port

I imagine being a sailor
two hundred years ago
free to wander round the town
no longer tied to bells
through its inns of welcome
and into fights and japes

when holds are filled
and stores of rum are stowed
with pay consumed
men are restive to be gone
yearning for the taste of salt
on a keening wind

I look again and see
a stand of Norfolk pines
those masts are trunks and stems
against the smoke filled air
the rest is reverie of what
I'd never spy.

The Siren

She walks a ragged coast
towards its unknown end
in her ears a call resounds
beyond the realm of time

she hears the ocean sing
of pearls and giant clams
where creatures of the deep
reside in terraces of kelp

she wants to hear it all
to enter that dark world
she does not fear the swell
the fishes or the seals

its music draws her in
songs echo through the brine
where caverns far from light
hold wonders yet unheard.

Selkie Skin

for Eunice

Cast off your water-tethered shell
and free the selkie waiting for this night
inside a timbered hull beneath the waterline
we gently peel into our human form

a flush of heat from deep within
releases pallid hide, exposing
all the tender parts, from feet to nape
and curving naked back
how shimmering you are

we lie entwined upon discarded fur
listen to each sound as men and women do
a slap of oily sea against the groaning wood
a kiss shaped breath from rising breast
your pulse and stretching limbs

we press our new found arms
I caress your skin, soft as a tear
clasp unfamiliar hands, explore
what fingers, tongues and toes can find
embrace the hours till dawn

awake to gulls and fisher wives
wind calling from the tackle overhead
before the sun we turn to seals again
must heed the warnings shown
go hunt the shoals and not attempt
to change for seven years

when close to shore
and rigging chatters in the dark
or soft waves slap against the wood
it's then I yearn and count the seasons down
to touch once more your silky unseal skin.

In Celtic mythology, the selkie is a seal who can shed their skin and transform into a human, but this can only occur once every seven years.

At Shippies

Home of the lauded race
a smell of cooking fat
slaps you in the nose
and from the galley comes
their famous battered fish

expectant smiles fill the bar
the regulars advance
wanting entertainment
they ply us for for a yarn
we jump ship, protest fatigue

like barnacles on neglected hulls
painted sailing ships, old prints
photographs of winning crews
encrust its rooms, halls, stairwells
no inch of space remains

they chart and celebrate
years of judging wind on seas
one summer week of fear and joy
no sleep with all that expectation
anchoring their lives

in our modest cabin
patient boats above the bed
wait for a breeze beyond their frame
crisp sheets festoon and fall
we sail on waves of sleep.

Ghosts

Battery Point flows down
to water lapping at its feet
shipwrights, crews and working men
are shadows on the roads

their cramped cottages
boast a whitewashed charm
preserve yesterday's uniform façade
small doors and window panes

backyards have been transformed
vast living rooms in open-plan
gaze out from walls of glass
to catch the views and light

old salts, the shades of years long gone
flit in and out, amuse themselves
play tricks with children's toys
a selling point in million-dollar real estate
poor workers once called home.

The Treasure Hunter

She finds sea-tumbled glass
as the tide retreats, holds it to the sun
a jewel in her hand

with child-like steps and hair dyed red
her floral skirt dragging in the sand
she's known to locals as Giddy Sal

she glues her finds onto the windowpane
morning sun slanting through the glass
transforms her walls to dancing lights

arms above her head she twirls
the doll, safe inside her jewellery box
revolving to its wind-up tune.

Catani Gardens

Beyond the tidal reach
marked by a grid of lines
tall palms, clipped grass
paths arrow shot
in neat municipal ways

here the rotunda stands
its centrepiece when new
the band played then speeches
welcomed dignitaries
straw-boatered pleasure seekers

now from the stage
cascades of shabby quilts
plastic bags strung across a line
they block our path
to the space she claims

once this land was coastal scrub
tea tree and sprawling banksia
home to her ancient rituals
the deep belonging
woven through this land

she no longer gathers mussels
from bay to dilly bag
those rituals have gone
she fishes nearby restaurants
for charity and scraps

between high-rent eateries
and the beat of fitness clubs
she sits, gets drunk and dreams
shouts abuse at us
before returning to her home.

Anzac Day

No crowds today
the brave, heads down
clutch jackets blown awry
mourn those who don't return

along our bay
each headland marked
a cenotaph looks out to sea
names those who don't return

once swathed in flowers
now a single wreath
is set upon the base
for those who don't return

so few remain
to march or mark this day
remember what was lost
by those who don't return.

Rye Back Beach

My parents owned a plot of land, an acre of sandy grass
low hills behind the dunes on the road to Cape Schank
it stretched forever to a nine-year-old and her younger brother

we drove from bland brick suburbs into timbered villages
beyond the trainline's end to small outposts with cedar verges
past long jetty land and convoluted tea tree scrub

as we stumbled out, there was nothing here to distinguish it
as ours, we struggled cross-country over bare dunes
slid, rolled down, grit in our mouths and into every crevice

the last dune slipped onto a wild ocean beach, untouched
by human footprints, the flotsam of storms flung into high
tide calligraphy of kelp, huge cuttlefish and bleaching shells

I trailed behind my mum, blown sideways by fierce wind
helped drag twisting driftwood she deemed as sculptural
at home it was arrayed on her chartreuse feature wall

I loved these abstracts, they inspired my passion for the
natural form, I studied art and became a sculptor but
Mum soured, she resented that I had the career she was denied.
Only now I understand all she sacrificed for us.

Survival Instinct

Waahn, the crow
totem of a tribe long gone
who called this bay their home

I hear your cry weigh the air
a shadow on the trees
as I walk my childhood beach

you know the story of this land
of fear, disease and bloody deaths
among the coastal scrub

the soft footprints of yesterday
brush shelter with a kindling fire
replaced by brick and stone

your diet of mussels, clams and mice
is now a smorgasbord of cafe scraps
from lanes and roadside bins

you watch our spinning days
with powerful wings and eyes
wait for the cycle's change.

Sand Between the Sheets

Luminous

As I reach the city outskirts
the light has changed
and my eyes adjust, open
to this southern sky

from wide diffusion
of hills and farms lit from above
to crystal bright, hard edged
now outlines dominate

sharp focused in concrete and steel
a super-realist painting of varied greys
even the machinery of docks
here everything glows

sun on the bay is an oblique spotlight
each boat poised on dancing water
the pier seems laser-cut
and burns its image on my heart.

Bella At Large

After the confines
of lockdown Blackheath
its cloud laden solitude
she finds herself exposed
to a cacophony of smells

on every post and tree, on masonry
stop-start walking to the beach
wind lifts her ears and nose
to seaweed on salt-blustered air
unfamiliar cries, dogs barking

running to the edge of fear
and back to me, the sights
of swimming, cycling, jogging
Sunday sounds at play
new friends to greet and sniff

leads tangle, legs everywhere
so much for she and I to see
to explore and mingle with
as waves of unfamiliar noise
break in every direction.

Opening Up, November 2021

Sunday morning on the street
the residue of Saturday night
its crowds and company
mac happy wrappers stitch the path
from tram to tourist beach

fallen masks and coffee cups
focus on the destination sought
where party groupies totter
single file, weave in and out of tables
to some promised bar

diners' plates with food piled high
and bubbling jugs of beer
gym-buffed types or podge and pale
they're making up for absence
here for all to see.

Luna Land

Painted mask, I see a heart
you always promised us diversion
beneath that gaping mouth

scaffolds arching through the air
there's derros pissing in the park
grey skies on blistered skin

we flock onto your stage
sand neatly raked, each day's a face
exposed and turned to please

with sugar hits and alcohol
against your peeling paint
we feast beyond excess

time's scored by ringing trams
a blur amid the glaring noise
that lures the tourists in

we soar and swoop, taste the lot
as each must play a part
Saint K, I'll be your pimp today.

St Kilda Summertime

Darkness comes round nine p.m.
squad car sirens pulse
like waves upon the shore
from Christ Church yard
fruit bat choirs
praise the god of figs

as parties spill into the street
bouncers marshal lines
for clubs above the shops
their music swells
until a truce of pre-dawn quiet
at six a.m. the garbage tanks roll in

morning is for dogs
they charge across the sand
while a grader spins its hulk
around the beach
pale tourists cruise for action
squint at the brazen light

breakfast coffee crews
move with a languid grace
straight back and sides men
sip from enviro cups
itching for a tram
eyes tuned to squares of screen

lorikeets outside old flats
squeal among the flowering gums
walkers dodging ground below
there's yoga at the park
where homeless men
glower from their sacks

at The Prince
old salts, the grizzled and the lank
muse into their beers
good-time girls and trans aflutter
ooze flesh from lycra skirts
as Harleys thunder in for drinks

this town of diverse haunts
where artists share the lows
and highs of shabby rent
with chancers, tarts and restaurants
no matter what the hour
I've always felt at home.

Bayside Vignette

Rubbish bins line the curb
overflow with retching smells
prawn shells rot in the heat
as holly-patterned paper
waves from yawning lids

there's no one on the streets
the flats are quiet
their residents are sleeping in
recovering from being nice
to everyone on Christmas Day

a large grey rat
saunters on the fence above
then edges to his buffet bar
pink ears and whiskers twitch
he's spoilt for choice today

I often see them here
as flat and desiccated corpses
swept to palm fronds in the shadows
or water-plump tied to weed
along the high tide mark

they occupy neglected spaces
stealthy raiders following our lives
some meet untimely ends
like us they thrive and fail
through baits and misadventure.

Acland Street Symphony

When the air is still
and cooling after dark
you can hear girls scream
at the other end of town
as they crest and dive
on the Scenic Railway

here in our stretch
the fruit bats squeal
squabbling over figs
and a spidery man
yells into his phone
about a deal gone wrong

the hari krishna troupe
prance beneath plane trees
banging on their drums
lads getting drunk
lean out of sweaty rooms
to mock or cheer them on

close by a solitary guitar
plies an unfamiliar chord
while in the flat next door
shouts with glasses thrown
build to crescendos of abuse
as another's music booms outside.

The Crime of Innocence

There is the bay and sunshine
on its rippling water
while he waits beneath the palms
watching walkers and their dogs
basking in a summer's morning

the tram dings into view
an innocent journey on his mind
as he slowly climbs aboard
thinking of the city and cafe
where he'll meet his sister

except a casual violence builds
in a brooding stranger
twitching for the chance to strike
choosing this disabled man
to scream at, punch him to the floor

with no other reason
than an easy target just appeared
while my brother in confusion
wonders through his shock and pain
what did he do, what was his crime.

On Ebb Tide

Like tides that come and go
our beach end of Fitzroy Street
turns derelict, unkempt
its crowds dwindle to regret

outside shops with pasted glass
and fading for-lease boards
the homeless come to sleep
indifferent to decline

as rubbish escalates
haunted men with jagged steps
and menace in their eyes
are hassling passers by

we scurry back to catch a tram
avoid the scrum ready for a fight
while further up the hill
blank offices transform

restaurants with hipster names
enjoy a new high tide, they beam
it's safe to be out late
here you can swim all night.

Urban Penguins

It's New Year in Melbourne
heat rises from the concourse
and the esplanade
from concrete shopping lanes

a lazy day gives up its light
lingers on in fiery clouds
the kiosk fades to silhouette
on its long jetty promenade

people crowd like black spears
upon the tumbled bluestone wall
they form a palisade of bodies
expectant, waiting for the sound

a splash then fleeting glimpse
of birds returning to their nests
and a city celebrates
the wildness at its heart.

Black Swan

No billabong or reed-edged lake
he arabesques beneath the pier
a red-beaked flag upon green swell

webbed feet against high winds
a head that dips between each wave
as night rolls down the sky

a duct tape label binds his neck
alone and close to shore
he tacks towards me on the sand

this urban dwelling, saltwater dancer
avoiding cars, sharp dogs and bikes
within a frame of flat and tower.

At the Turn

The sea flows out
ankle deep in shallows
seagulls take their places
silent, poised, alert

the birds begin to dance
speed tapping in a row
dislodging clams and crabs
caught on a falling tide

the sand is strung with hollows
slowly drying in the sun
from agile line dancers
stepping to the beat.

In Homage

Early mornings at the park   solitary
on the beach, down tree-lined streets
they come, old women with their dogs
who trail behind   sniffing at a tree
or sweating mound of sand

the women bend arthritic hips and knees
once lithe enough to dance all night
now they pick a line   gather rubbish
discarded bottles, wrappers, masks
fill their bag   dump in a bin and leave

no self conscious act seeking praise
this simple ritual   care and respect
is a meditation, healing as a yoga class
for the heart   their gift to mother earth
each day this dance of love repeats.

Yachts

Translucent in the haze
they float as wings
above a fading canvas
sea and air not blue or white
but something in between

as if an artist with her paints
once chose vermilion and chrome
bright cobalt for the sky
but that was many years ago
the colours now have leached

exposed too long in the sun
her art is lost to pallid hues
what's left are ghostly shapes
languid with no wind
late afternoon in saturated heat.

Flightless Birds

The day begins in oven heat
drags on above mid-forties
with deserted streets and cabin fever
we swelter, drowse, complain

at dusk the change arrives
now the city promenades
a brisk wind chops the bay
dark shapes in fading light

kite-surfers rise and tack
fly across the waves
cyclists weave through crowds
strolling to the pier

we remember youth's dexterity
as we slump into a seat
there's nothing to be proved
once we soared like them.

Painting the Morning

Beneath my toes
the crunch of shell grit sand
fragments of coking coal and brick

with fresh dog prints
lit by the rising sun
we dance into our shadows' stretch

a grader thumps
begins its daily sweep
swings past our wandering steps

erases signs of yesterday
life's abstract on the beach
another's lost moments in the sun

it leaves the canvas blank
for my dog and I to print
our shared delight of running free.

Bright Bella

Against the blanching cold
she's coated tight
but the wind's a whip
upon her face

seaweed strands
hurled onto the beach
sand still soft, her paws
sink deep and damp

low tide's expanse
a blur of amber grains
where shallow pools
reflect the darkening clouds

a high-speed prance
despite her aged bones
with tail held high
the small grown bold

her dash to distance
and recall, beyond
the bleakness
of this wintery day.

Salt on the Skin

The bay curls towards us
falls back, repeats the invitation
to slip our land locked feet
and embrace its liquid mystery

translucent layers shift
aqua blue in bands of green
rippling through the shallows
that caress its sun warmed sand

fish are silver shadows
these agile threads of life
dart through seaweed fingers
retreat to greater depths

we enter the water, surrender
know its timeless body
holds us buoyant as a grey gull
that floats on soft wave breaths.

Homesong

Standing on the pier
my long walk to its edge
stung by shearing winds
or wilting in the sun
I listen to a slap of waves

here fairy penguins make their home
and gulls from further south are seen
the palisade of masts, a curtain
drawn across the city outline
its symphony of greys
buildings rise low to high

in misted soft or strident notes
the music of my town is heard
through years of boom and bust
football crowds and rattling trams
of crows and lorikeets
as cafés on the street spread out
or shrink to silent caves.

Waterworn

The Riverside Path

Sound laps the Wingecarribee
with trumpet blasts of cockatoos
and upward lilts from currawongs

the arching grace of heron wings
above dense rush and blackberry
dun-coloured water pocked by rain
peeling gums release their scent

walkers hold a measured pace
the drizzle and the cold dispelled
in warm exchanges as we pass

this time we make to be absorbed
beyond our busy streetside world
here lives are free to move
at their wild nature's call

to hear the river as it rolls
over rocks and pebble grit
and lose ourselves in timelessness.

The River of Cloud

From its source
in volcanic zones of fire and steam
above jungles dense with heat
it stretches wide and long

it is greater than the Amazon
but here no fish can thrive
flowing to the east
across the ocean plains
pushing north and south
beyond where birds can fly

when the river meets warm land
a cliff or mountain range
it must disgorge as rain
falling to the thirsty land
this mighty weight
turns earth to seas of mud.

Nowhere to Run

The east coast of our land
submits to climate change
we surrender   our homes
our towns and livelihoods
the rivers flood, swallow drivers
in their swirling waters

while we on higher ground
are watching   warm and dry
left to imagine what it's like
for the family with small children
or us, the old, to spend the dark
alone with no power or phone

trapped by torrential rain
on a roof   or in its cavity
as the waters spin and surge
lift chairs, table and the fridge
a red-brown sea filled with debris
oozing, flowing, rising to our fears.

La Serenissima Protests

She's had enough of cruising behemoths
rejects the gawking crowds
I felt her cold shoulder many years ago

nuns shush us from the pews in San Marco
flooded by ship's wash on their lagoon
there's no room for locals in the Bridge of Sighs
priced out of homes and espresso bars

they grumble as we stop their daily work
we hover, snap them reinforcing walls
as her ancient pylons sink deeper in the mud

we love this city of crooked palaces
her peeling majesty weighed down by age
the world knows Venice is drowning, still
we want to wave her off before she goes.

Yesterday's Ocean

Today I'm with a little boy
who's eager for the aquarium
he skips along, can barely wait
for all the fish there'll be to see

he loves them all
at five he knows their names
the shapes and iridescent
colour of their scales

he knows the taste of some
from cuttlefish that cling
and bream upon his line
he wants to learn what else there is

from monster sharks up close
to tiny spines and fantailed fish
how delicate a seahorse is
and the grace of manta rays

there's a danger he can't know –
who would spoil his innocence?
the ocean and its wonders
is warming as he grows.

Jellyfish

Salt water pulse
valves in and out   in and out   and on
coloured stripes   red yellow black   blend or clear
long tentacles stretch   drift and pull   death sting on touch
and from their bloom of eggs   a billion-fold increase
bellows puff   deflate   push against the depths
seas rise and warm   fish stocks decline
till all we have to eat
is slime.

The Lone Sailor

Distance is a constant point
above the toss of ocean swell
when ports are weeks apart

his eyes grow hard
on wind-sheared sea and sky
he looks for birds drawn to his sail

no albatross or shark cruise by
once there were dolphin pods
that cut his wake like scimitars

debris shoals now ride the waves
anchor fish and birds to starve
he navigates through a raft of bones.

The Grindadrap

Pilot whales come north
Faroe's men in boats
are waiting for the pod
driving them ashore
to launch their annual kill
inside a ring of blood

refugees come south
lives made unbearable
driven from their homes
meet border guards in boats
women, children, men
forced into offshore camps

whales and refugees
are trapped, one group
is killed with spinal lance
quickly as they can
the other slowly going mad
inside our ring of steel.

Mohad's Anniversary

The decision
no other could be made
a youngest son
no wife to halt my feet

the debt I own
feels like a baited hook
I pray a better life
will cut me free again

I wait my turn
how slow the journey out
slow the truck and van
and then a dreadful boat

trapped in the hold
like fish we gasped for air
choked by the dark
and biting diesel fumes

a larger engine throbs
to sounds of yells
we board another ship
are given food and hope

today marks seven years
though time means little here
lost souls strung on the line
of this detention camp.

From Her Window

Three hundred whales
pass by here each day
no longer prey to hunters
we have halted their decline

she watches but a few
those who signal with a breach
or crash of tail
as she stands looking out

they are her talisman
against the aching year
one short respite
when she can hold
the rhythms of the sea.

Hermit Rocks

Small outcrops off the coast
close enough to swim to
a beacon for reclusive souls
the refuge for my jangled spirit

I crave a deep sea sky
the pulse and slap of waves
to soothe unruly currents
when the mind's worn haggard

I'd build a hutch, a shelter
from rock wall and drifted wood
secure against the rising tide
that offers respite from a gale

my plot of hardy weeds to tend
an oil lamp and warm dog
a little boat for escape
should melancholy overwhelm

this dream of cosy island hovel
a hideaway from bad weather
alas no island can exclude
the storms that rage in my head.

Through Another Art

I am ironing a length of silk
vibrant colours dominate
splashed light and dark
my arm sweeps back and forth

the rhythm carries me
like wings above the cloth
an eagle's view of far below
green islands in a tropic sea

surrounded by turquoise lagoons
the sun sweats tangerine to red
blurs borders, glare magnifies
I retreat to shading palms

an ocean breeze cools my eyes
in respite from the heat
along the hand rolled edge
clouds bank dark grey

a storm at the horizon's rim
that never closes in
I cruise an archipelago
led by the artist's hand.

Big Rivers

Here rivers glide
through vast alluvial plains
ease towards a dimpled range
this fat rumped land
where paperbarks and she oaks
drain saturated ground

the furthest bank
blue-hazed by distance
where cow sheds slump and rust
enclosed in vines
the dairy herds abandoned
beef cattle fatten on lush pasture

the road sharp cut
between long squares of green
hemmed in or opening out
all roads lead to the refinery
it's bathed in smoke
a sickly sweetness on the air

late afternoon canefields
swathed in bands of river mist
a butcher-bird's refrain
scrolls through Bangalow palms
fills coastal towns
dozing in their warmth.

The Ugly Duckling Tree

Called the screw pine
even its name is strident
with an architecture prehistoric
reptilian in appearance

a truss of roots and spiky leaves
bulwark against encroaching waves
binds sandy streets and verge
in coastal gardens of the north

this warty remnant dinosaur
used as medicine and food
our shelter for millennia
thatched hut, bird sanctuary

fruit ripens into orange drupes
abundant stores of energy
for fruit bats and rats to spread
this golden goose of trees.

The Tropic of Contrasts

Waking to the sound of waves
buffeting an ocean beach
a riff of notes outside my room
the butcher-bird's song of light
calls me to rise and swim

now the ocean burns in sunset
and a seamist clouds the land
lorikeets squabble through the trees
from the restaurant below
scents of spice and garlic rise

the sky turns shades of pearl
seen through palm frond stripes
I sit and muse on this sojourn
far from my mountain home
of dawn and dusk enchantment
and roasting hours between.

This Moment, a Breath

Inhale the breeze
it is a traveller through our land
past desert and deep valleys
above the great dividing spine
down to my thirsting lungs

exhale into the ocean
how many hours and days
this echo from my body
to Chile's western shore
its mountains wreathed in snow

I breathe the sky, the earth and trees
the rivers and the creeks
cast them to roll on waves' infinity
through mighty lungs of whale
or cresting dolphin's break

a part of this great cycle
connecting every creature
through tropics to the ice caps
in a constant blending motion
the breath of life on earth.

Sea Steps

My pulse beats with the waves
that settle on a shingle beach
tumbling words inside my head

like stones among the sand
my thoughts begin to rub
sorting rough from smooth

I'm looking for the path
ragged lines that I can walk
back through the tides of years

to where I stand today
in making sense of self
the storms that rise and ebb.

Listing to Port

Aquamarine

Two days on the road
through country towns and flood plains
from twists and rise of mountain pass
of forests in the clouds   down
round and round the spiral unwinds
to farmland's endless sprawl

a motel break and then
another day matching lines to tar
my destination   a multistoreyed
eagle's eye of ocean to horizon span
my first impulse, draw curtains wide
open terrace doors   and breathe

inhale the shallows tinged with green
and murderous purple reefs
a narrow channel cutting through
hemmed by basalt breakwalls
guiding boats into the port
their safe anchorage and home

this is what I've ached for
I trace the line of ocean beach
spray curving into distance
to the headland far away
my heart's tight knot releases
anchored in aquamarine.

Time Share

i.

Like a pelican unfurling wings
I crave the ozone in my lungs
to leave a winter closely bound
and stretch my limbs in salted air

each year since we were newly wed
the road will take us north
redeem that one short week
bought on the apex of our love

I stop the car to ease my back
a stranger looks me in the eye
pit black, the crow stands its ground
beside a house submerged in vines

the bird gives out a strangulated cry
filled with the breadth of country it may span
when wings unleash their strength
beyond this willow flooded creek

for now it's parked on guard
I bow, acknowledge him the ruler of this land
retreat and slowly wheel away.

ii.

Shopkeepers age like us, the town spreads
down the coast and into hinterland
where vineyard galleries expand
with more resorts amid retiree zones

homes increase their palm tree fringe
I note the scrub once lush and dense
is now red sand for winnowing
as another complex grows

the perfect surfside resting place
between Sydney and Gold Coast
where old folks cast their final lines
put new roots into sand

today I'm ageless like the sky
below me rides blue on endless blue
the view I missed for all last year
through stifled covid months, is here.

Sunday Notebook

The water's stitched by shadows
surfers wait in silvered light
they hold each rise and fall
sliding past their boards
for time's their own today

a slow procession glides
beyond the sea wall's mouth
sails, translucent moth wings
each held taut, straining for
the starter's gun, their hearts to race

a man of flexed intent
pours bursts of energy
up and down a cliff of stairs
counts time in heaving breaths
his goal, destress for fitness sake

midday and the town
fills with parents and their kids
I watch these family groups
from market rounds to games
and picnics on the Green

this place of holidays
of campers by the sea
the tourists come and go
today the local office folk
take off their shoes and play.

Basking

Silver, dove and steel grey
the shades of sea and sky
a soft capped swell
beneath the stippled clouds

today water floats into the sky
lost in mist and rain
with no distinction
just the murmuring of waves

breakers billow like silk curtains
when the sun shines free
a shimmer of green and purple depth
then the ocean turns to steel again

the streets sluiced clean
from days of heavy rain
birds emerge, reclaim their territory
plovers squawk as we sidle past

our lazy moods of late age holidays
beach breakfasts in the lee of wind
like gulls we bunch, gusts of laughter
spilling over morning walkers

our gentle promenades
as youngsters power-walk ahead
this time when we rekindle dreams
in places loved, not as home

but better for brief hours spent
of feeling younger than we are
for who we could have been
beach bums and vagabonds.

Friday's Beach

School's out
and it's a balmy 24 degrees
on this midwinter coast
an untidy headland at one end
tumbles to the break

a host of low-tide rock pools
amid the hard-ridged stone
cruel on tender feet
but children scramble in abundance
ducking from the waves

they search and yell
when something live is found
these miniature worlds
where anemones wave
and abruptly close if poked

I remember being just like them
so many years ago
the wonder of strange creatures
that lived in briny water
trapped with no way out

and how I watched with horror
when my brother found a stick
prodded the small animal
to see how fast it shrank.

At Shelly Beach

We share our stories
scratch a picture in the sand
that other eyes will find

here there is a sculpture
of complex beauty
in driftwood, stones and shell
made with an artist's hand

the sculptor left her work
to nature's whim
for tide to mould and wind dissolve

children descend
hang off its fire-turned beams
dislodge the parts and patterning
fill its negatives with sand

the children's game has made
an abstract I can't read
the wind and waves will come
create this work anew.

Stepping Into Shadows

Saturday night fills the streets
here every restaurant is booked out
music pumps from cafés, bars and utes
while cars and bikes power up the hill

the town's high-wired tonight
laughter rises from pavement tables
with scents of smoke and sizzling meats
along the seaside belt

come Monday night at eight
I step outside to walk the dog
now a wall of absence meets me
even the waves have fallen mute

an eerie darkness fogs the town
I sense the ghosts of its colonial heart
are free to wander here again
as something chill brushes past my skin.

The Stations of My Day

The numinous takes many forms –

The sun still low, a breeze soft blown
before a heating day exhausts
desire to walk the distance
my yoga – air bathing on the shore

all along the breakwall ridge
fishermen display their catch
spend lives in salty dreaming
tugging on their lines

the stretch of Town Beach sand
with drifted wood on high tide shifts
that wind-shorn trees entangle
each one a life to contemplate

here surfers meditate in waves
on the ocean's measured beat
then waddle up the bank
peel wetsuit skins in time for work

one hour to reach the kiosk
I order, sit and face the beach
bright voices bank and dive
where friendship's bond is sacred

clouds build, the ocean softens
on the breakers' tumbling edge
a blue-green vibrance shimmers
hours pass in veneration.

Entering the Depths

I listen to the sea
its keening pulse, imagine
the constant heave and suck
of sand and tumbled shells
rolling into fragments
building seabed plains

the weight and energy
of waves that never cease
hurling nets of sinuous weed
far flung trees and stones
carried from the depths
towards each waiting shore

dunes rise, collapse, rebuild
erase the cliffs of yesterday
or silt a river's mouth
what lies buried underneath
are stories to be read, this reverie
is my treasure map to dreams.

The Sighting

I'm looking out to sea
bathed in light and warmth
deep aquamarine waves
dimple to the horizon

a flash of white and spume
the spray no boat could make
unsure if it's illusion
my eyes are slow to focus

beneath the curved horizon
I squint against the glare
calculate the distance
where I might see a plume

one great splash of breaching tail
as this young whale cavorts
and my spirit swells
to fill the ocean wide.

Echoes

The ocean is muffled by haze
a fading sun casts lilac tones
on walls, the sea and boats
time lingers between day and night

their hours of foraging end
lorikeets return on waves of noise
and the coastal pines darken
branches weighed by birds

they watch for mates to land
then roost in silent pairs
the harbour stills to reflection
streets are hushed tonight

at sunrise clouds of parrots leave
the trees resume sparse silhouettes
in sheltered hollows on the ground
hosts of tiny feathers fill
with bright echoes of their flight.

Oriole

The curve of wing at rest
is compact as a folded fan
it opens wide as she ascends
towards the canopy of figs

steady in long distance beats
above the rise of coastal hills
her eyes scan up and down
wary of a raptor strike

she has endured hard years
with drought, then fires
now flooded lands
unsure if she will nest again

the roost with voices of her kind
calling in the fading light
safe for now
to fold her head and wings.

Heart to Heart

Birds catch their breath
on leeward balconies
I watch two magpies mate
oblivious to the gale

these lives of seasonal change
of pairing, nesting, parenting
like us but strange, their fragile
impulse driven minds

at times we harmonise
they come to us for food
settle for our scraps
or seeds that we provide

tonight they jockey for a roost
each tree a shaking host
their calls murmuring to quiet
now snuggled in for sleep

together by the ocean
we hear the beat of waves
tolling through the dark
each heart is pacing down its hours.

Waterborne

The towns is bright, sun ripened, opening to warmth
rain cleansed and clipped hedge streets, people shop
come out to dine, they walk the breakwall with their
dogs as children skate and cycle round and round.
Passing tourists say, the place has changed somehow.

Last year, fire in surrounding hills scorched townsfolk's
lungs with smoke, people watched walls of flame ravage
farms and livestock, seared open their hearts, they wept
to see koalas burn in trees. A short respite, to catch their
breath and count the loss, accept, no one is safe from a
changing climate. Too soon rivers became deadly, rose
and rose beyond their feared predictions, they drowned
north shore homes as mudslides closed the roads and
highway, restaurants and shops deluged, saw livelihoods
abandoned. The once laid-back lifestyle now has an edge
of wariness and grief, caught in locals' eyes and bearing.

Beaches tell the story, reminding all who come, each
stretch of sand and foreshore decked in high-tide waves
of splintered wood on tumbled and eroded cliffs. Whole
trees and building timber heaped among the weed and
grass, marked by fire and flood, here no one can forget.

Bench Marks

A small brass plaque set in wood
holds the name and years they lived
in their child or parent's memory

I walk between each one, sit down
and listen to the churn of waves
bird calls and working men

I mark the stations of remembered lives
take in the scenes from cliff and bend
fill my eyes with views they loved.

Ozone

It feels so good to walk on sand
a sound of ocean waves
breaking at the shore
I hear them fall and taste the air
where lungs can hold their fill

the spread of shells and salted wood
shards of glass and stones worn smooth
to name them as I walk; green serpentine
red jasper veined and cloudy quartz
along the high-tide skein

head down, eyes pick the line
I kneel, examine what is found
roll them in my hand, hold towards the sun
collecting for the image in my head
of mobiles and assemblages

an angel with a heart of burnished stone
soft driftwood arms and legs
a flight of birds on green glass wings
banded shells and barnacles
expanding to mandala wheels

enough to see them in my head
sculptures for imaginary walls
the art that will not live
I leave the beach with empty hands
a heart that's filled with light.

Love Token

Waves lap my head with sound
cool beneath my skin
I wade a pool of stones
search for the heart shaped one
to hang above our bed

you will hold me close
tell me how a youthful Earth
pressed, bent and fused hard rock
before the ocean wore it down
cast us this smooth heartstone.

www.ingramcontent.com/pod-product-compliance
Lightning Source LLC
Chambersburg PA
CBHW070307120526
44590CB00017B/2584